Dave the Potter

ARTIST, POET, SLAVE

By LABAN CARRICK HILL
Illustrated by BRYAN COLLIER

L B

LITTLE, BROWN AND COMPANY
New York   Boston

*T*o us
it is just dirt,

the ground we walk on.

Scoop up a handful.

The gritty grains slip

between your fingers.

On wet days,
heavy with rainwater,
it is cool and squishy,
mud pie heaven.

But to Dave
it was clay,
the plain and basic stuff
upon which he learned to
form a life
as a slave nearly
two hundred years ago.

To us
it is just a pot,
round and tall,
good for keeping
marbles
or fresh-cut flowers.

But to Dave,
it was a pot
large enough to store
a season's grain harvest,
to put up salted meat,
to hold memories.

Each one began

out of clouds of dust,

clotted clumps of clay

ground in the pug mill and carried,

wheelbarrow after wheelbarrow,

to Dave's spinning potter's wheel.

With a flat wooden paddle
large enough to row
across the Atlantic,
Dave mixed clay with water
drawn from Big Horse Creek,
until wet and stiff and heavy.

He threw the clay,
sometimes sixty pounds at once,
and nobody knew
how or where it would land
except for Dave.

Dave kicked
his potter's wheel
until it spun
as fast as
a carnival's wheel of fortune.

Like a

magician

pulling

a rabbit

out of

a hat,

Dave's hands, buried
in the mounded mud,
pulled out the shape of a jar.

His chapped thumbs
pinched into the center,
squeezed the inside
against his fingers outside.

As the wheel spun

round and round,

the walls of the jar

rose up like a robin's

puffed breast—

but only so far

before its immense weight

threatened collapse.

The jar grew so large

Dave could no longer

wrap his strong arms around it.

If he climbed into the jar

and curled into a ball,

he would have been embraced.

Only then did he
stop his potter's wheel
and roll long ropes
of clay between
his dry, caked palms.

Dave mounted
these coils of clay
one by one
on the half-finished jar.
He ran his wet fingers
along the sides to smooth
it all together,
kicking the wheel
with the heel of his foot.

The shoulder and rim

shrugged upward

as the jar took the shape

Dave knew was there,

even before he worked

the raw mound on his wheel.

While the clay dried,
Dave pounded
wood ash and sand
to mix a glasslike
brown glaze
to withstand time.

But before the jar
completely hardened,
Dave picked up a stick
and wrote to let us know
that he was here.

I wonder where
is all my relation
friendship to all—
and, every nation

I wonder where is all my relation
friendship to all—and, every nation

Aug 16, 1857 Dave

Five works by Dave the potter.

Dave: A life

I wonder where is all my relation
friendship to all—and, every nation
                              —*August 16, 1857*

Dave is an important American artist. His beautifully crafted jars stand out among the pottery of the time. His whimsical poems embody a simplicity and deep emotional complexity that rivals Japanese haiku. These are remarkable accomplishments in themselves, but for Dave, who lived most of his life as a slave, they are even more incredible. We have printed his poems here as they appeared on the pots, including "mistakes" as well as various marks such as dashes and plus signs. As Leonard Todd states in *Carolina Clay*, "With so few words surviving from this gifted and unusual person, almost alone in his role of slave witness, it's important for us to get them right." Dave created his art in spite of a society that not only discouraged his brilliance but threatened him with death for expressing it.

We know about Dave mainly because of what he wrote on his pottery. For long periods of time, Dave did not write on the sides of his pots, perhaps because he knew it was not safe. He would sometimes just sign his name. He only had a first name because slaves were not allowed to have family names, like "Hill" or "Collier." Other times he might put the date. Once in a while he would include a poem. Perhaps he wrote his poems for a specific person, or maybe for just anyone who could read.

put every bit all between
surely this Jar will hold 14
—July 12, 1834

This poem was written on one of the earliest pots that we know for certain Dave made. It tells us that the pot can hold fourteen gallons. Dave was one of only two known potters at the time who could successfully make pots that were larger than twenty gallons, sometimes as large as forty gallons. To do this he had to wrestle more than sixty pounds of clay on his turning wheel, a feat that required great skill and strength.

Dave belongs to Mr. Miles /
wher the oven bakes & the pot biles ///
—July 31, 1840

Some of what we know about Dave is buried in the shadows of the lives of his owners. The first record of Dave dates to his seventeenth year. His name appeared on a contract to borrow money to buy a house. Because his age is mentioned, we know that he was born sometime around 1801. We also learn that he was born in the United States, but we don't know where.

a better thing, I never saw
when I shot off, the lions Jaw
—November 9, 1836

We can suppose that Dave lived a life much better than that of most slaves who worked in the fields. As a potter, he had a skill few black people were allowed to learn. Slaves were generally used for unskilled jobs. White slave owners feared that if their slaves learned skills such as blacksmithing or pottery, they might demand freedom and respect. For the same reason, slaves were not allowed to learn to read and write. How Dave learned may never be known.

another trick is worst than this +
Dearest miss: spare me a Kiss +
                              —*August 26, 1840*

According to Leonard Todd, Dave lost his leg when he was around thirty-five years old. After that, his friend Henry, whose arms were crippled, kicked the potter's wheel for him. The details of the story in this book are taken from Dave's life before and after he lost his leg, but the focus is on Dave as a potter and poet. With this in mind, the facts surrounding Dave's lost leg were not included.

when you fill this Jar with pork or beef
Scot will be there; to Get a peace,—
                              —*April 21, 1858*

We do know that some of Dave's poems leave a smile, while others offer observations on his life.

the sun moon and—stars=
in the west are a plenty of—bears "'
                              —*July 29, 1858*

Over the years, Dave's poems shared the pain of losing his family as well as his love for others. His words expressed his humanity, his compassion, and his own passion for life. According to Jill Beute Koverman in *I Made This Jar . . .*, it is estimated that over seven decades Dave made approximately forty thousand pots, but it is only through these few surviving poems that we get to know him. The last surviving jar inscribed with a poem is dated May 3, 1862. This poem is a fitting epitaph for Dave.

I, made this Jar, all of cross
If, you dont repent, you will be, lost=

AUTHOR'S NOTE

In 2003, I attended a conference on the Middle Passage organized by Dr. Lorrie Smith at St. Michael's College in Vermont. Toward the end of the day, I wandered into a talk being given by Dr. Lisa Gail Collins, a professor of art at Vassar College. Her presentation was on African influences on African American art. At one point during the talk, she showed an image of a pot with a poem written on it. She very briefly described the pot, read the poem ("I, made this Jar, all of cross/ If, you don't repent, you will be, lost="), and explained that an African American slave named Dave had made the pot. I left that conference with Dave's poem resonating in my head. For a year I thought about Dave and his poem. One evening, while I was watching PBS's *Antiques Roadshow*, a pot made by Dave appeared. As the antiques dealer described the value of the pot, I began to think more about Dave's poems. As I began to research Dave online, I discovered that there had been an exhibition of Dave's pots at the McKissick Museum at the University of South Carolina in 1998. The McKissick had published an exhibition catalog. Jill Beute Koverman, a graduate student in art history, had curated the show and collected in the exhibition catalog all the material known about Dave. At this point, I began to write my own poem to celebrate Dave's life and art. This picture book is an expression of my great admiration for and awe of Dave as an artist, a poet, and a potter.

—Laban Carrick Hill

ILLUSTRATOR'S NOTE

During my research for this book, I learned that the enslaved potter named Dave had lived in an area just outside Edgefield, South Carolina—Pottersville. And so I made my way down to South Carolina to see for myself the ground that Dave walked on. Once in Edgefield, I was directed to the studio of a local potter named Stephen Ferrell. Mr. Ferrell explained to me that Dave the potter is a central figure in the rich history of pottery made in the Carolinas. He then proceeded to throw a pot before my very eyes. He also showed me an authentic jar signed and dated by Dave that was displayed in his studio.

The watercolor/collage images for this book depict Dave engaged in the step-by-step process of creating pottery, from extracting the clay from the earth to grinding, kneading, and preparing the clay for the wheel, to applying the ash glaze. Finally, Dave handwrites a poetic verse on the outside of the jar, adding the date and his signature. Because there are no known visual references showing what Dave actually looked like, I based my illustrations on a model who I felt reflected the spirit of Dave. Throughout this book, certain images remind the reader that Dave was a slave—images of shackles and chains, and of slaves picking cotton in the fields. In many ways, Dave's artistry may have served as his own glimpse of freedom, and a way of carving out a life under the brutal and dehumanizing conditions of slavery. Dave's noble jars and verses blaze through the ages and speak profoundly of dignity to our generation and beyond.

—Bryan Collier

BIBLIOGRAPHY

Ceramic Art of North Carolina. CD-ROM. The Mint Museum of Art, Charlotte, NC.

Kohl, MaryAnn F. *Mudworks: Creative Clay, Dough and Modeling Experiences.* Bellingham, WA: Bright Ring Publishing, 1989.

Koverman, Jill Beute, ed. *I Made This Jar . . . The Life and Works of the Enslaved African-American Potter, Dave.* Columbia, SC: McKissick Museum, 1998.

The Mint Museum of Art Teacher Resource Posters, Charlotte, NC: The Mint Museum of Art, 2000.

Pottery, Poetry, and Politics, Surrounding the Enslaved African-American Potter, Dave. Symposium. McKissick Museum, the University of South Carolina, April 25, 1998.

Todd, Leonard. *Carolina Clay: The Life and Legend of the Slave Potter Dave.* New York: W.W. Norton, 2008.

Zug, Charles G. *Turners and Burners: The Folk Potters of North Carolina.* Chapel Hill, NC: University of North Carolina Press, 1986.

WEBSITES

An educator's guide to Dave: www.digitaltraditions.net/html/D_Resources.cfm

Online biography of Dave: www.usca.edu/aasc/davepotter.htm

Website of Dave biographer Leonard Todd: www.leonardtodd.com

Photograph of five works by Dave the potter: Storage jar, 1840, Collection of Dr. and Mrs. James
K. Smith; pitcher, 1850, and two storage jars, 1857, Collection of McKissick Museum; jug, ca.
1857–59, Collection of Larry and Joan Carlson. Photograph by Gordon Brown and Jill Beute
Koverman. All rights reserved, McKissick Museum, University of South Carolina.

Little, Brown and Company • Hachette Book Group • 237 Park Avenue, New York, NY 10017
Visit our website at www.lb-kids.com
Little, Brown and Company is a division of Hachette Book Group, Inc.
The Little, Brown name and logo are trademarks of Hachette Book Group, Inc.

The publisher is not responsible for websites (or their content) that are not owned by the publisher.

Library of Congress Cataloging-in-Publication Data

Hill, Laban Carrick.
    Dave the potter / by Laban Carrick Hill ; illustrated by Bryan Collier. —1st ed.
       p. cm.
    ISBN 978-0-316-10731-0
    1. Dave, fl. 1834–1864—Juvenile literature. 2. African American potters—Biography—
Juvenile literature. 3. African American poets—Biography—Juvenile literature. 4. Slaves—South
Carolina—Biography—Juvenile literature. I. Collier, Bryan, ill. II. Title.
    NK4210.D247H55 2010
    738.092—dc22
    [B]
                                        2010006382

First Edition: September 2010 • ISBN: 978-0-316-10731-0
6 7 8 9 10 • SC • Printed in China

The illustrations for this book were done in watercolor/collage on 400lb Arches watercolor paper.
The text was set in Berylium, and the display type is Aquiline.

For Lorrie Smith and Jennifer Hunt, both of whom made this book possible.

—L.C.H.

I dedicate this book to all artists, and everyone who loves picture books.

Because this story is really about the power of the human spirit, artistry, and truth,

and that cannot be silenced by bondage of any kind.

—B.C.